FOR THE SAKE OF THE KINGDOM

Publishers of *For the Sake of the Kingdom*

Australia

Anglican Information Office
St Andrew's House
Sydney Square
Sydney 2000

Canada

Anglican Book Centre
600 Jarvis Street
Toronto, Ontario M4Y 2J6

Ghana

Anglican Printing Press
PO Box 8
Accra

Kenya

Uzima Press Ltd
PO Box 48127
Nairobi

New Zealand

Genesis
29 Westminster Street
PO Box 22–537
Christchurch

Nigeria

CSS Press
50 Broad Street
PO Box 174
Lagos

Southern and Central Africa

Collins Liturgical Publications
Distributed in Southern
Africa by
Lux Verbi, PO Box 1822
Cape Town 8000

Tanzania

Central Tanganyika Press
PO Box 15
Dodoma

Uganda

Centenary Publishing House
PO Box 2776
Kampala

United Kingdom

Church House Publishing
Church House
Great Smith Street
London SW1P 3NZ

United States of America

Forward Movement Publications
412 Sycamore Street
Cincinnati, Ohio 45202

**Inter-Anglican Theological
and Doctrinal Commission**

FOR THE SAKE
OF THE KINGDOM
God's Church and the New Creation

PUBLISHED FOR THE
ANGLICAN CONSULTATIVE COUNCIL

Published 1986 for the Anglican Consultative Council
14 Great Peter Street, London SW1P 3NQ
by the publishers listed opposite the title page.

This edition by
Church House Publishing,
Church House, Great Smith Street
London SW1P 3NZ

ISBN 0 7151 7305 7

Printed by THE PRINT BUSINESS LTD London SE19 2TA

Contents

Preface

It was at the third meeting of the Anglican Consultative Council in Trinidad in 1976 that the idea was conceived of a representative commission to consider theological and doctrinal questions which concern the Anglican Communion as a whole. The proposal was endorsed by the 1978 Lambeth Conference, and the Inter-Anglican Theological and Doctrinal Commission was subsequently established.

The Commission was given its initial brief by the Anglican Consultative Council in these terms:

> Church and Kingdom in Creation and Redemption, being a study of the relationship between the Church of God as experienced and the Kingdom of God as anticipated, with special reference to the diverse and changing cultural contexts in which the Gospel is proclaimed, received, and lived.

The Commission met three times, in England (1981), Barbados (1983), and Ireland (1985). In each place we were warmly received by the local church and these contacts formed a significant part of the context of our discussions. We continued our work between each ten-day meeting by correspondence, and members contributed a wide range of papers, the titles of which are listed in Appendix 1. Copies of these papers are available at the ACC office. As the Commission's work developed, responses were elicited from a number of provincial doctrinal commissions and individual theologians around the Anglican Communion. These responses contributed considerably to our work.

The Commission was not established to be – and would itself firmly disclaim any pretensions to being – a supreme authority for the Anglican Communion on disputed questions of doctrine. Such a role would not accord with our

Anglican understanding of 'dispersed authority'. Nor have we tried to tackle the host of specific theological questions which are 'biting' around the world. This Report has a more modest aim: to suggest a broad framework of theological understanding within which the answers to more specific questions can be developed.

Inevitably this gives the Report a somewhat abstract character. Nevertheless we believe it proposes principles which are applicable to many of the questions that trouble different churches of our Communion. It will, however, need 'translation' into the terms of local questions and circumstances. This can only be done at local level, and we hope that each of the churches of the Anglican Communion will make its own 'translation', bringing to the Report its own questions and illuminating it with its own stories. The Report is to be part of the background material of the 1988 Lambeth Conference, and we hope it has a useful contribution to make. That will only be true to the extent that each diocese and Province takes seriously the application of the Report to its own pressing theological concerns.

Every member of the Commission has made his or her own distinctive contribution to our work, and it would be invidious to single out individuals. It should be said, however, that we are particularly indebted to the creative contribution of Bishop Lakshman Wickremesinghe, who died before our third meeting. His personal struggle with the question of what it means to be a Christian in a culture shaped by another great world religion and in a context of oppression of minorities gave an urgency to our discussions which kept us aware of the life-and-death reality of the issues with which we were wrestling.

All our members would testify to the richness of cross-cultural dialogue in the Commission. We are not all professional theologians, and such value as the Report has will reflect as much the results of the interplay of insights from the diversity of our worldwide Communion as the theological expertise of individual members. Perhaps that in itself says something of the way in which the Holy Spirit leads the Church into truth.

KEITH RAYNER
Chairman

1 Introduction

The Commission's Task

1   During the last ten or fifteen years, the Anglican Communion has become increasingly aware that it needs to form a common mind on a variety of pressing theological and doctrinal issues. These issues have been posed partly by ecumenical dialogues and partly by theological movements that have grown out of modern social, political, and economic developments in many parts of the world. In particular, increasing contact between the church and non-Christian cultures has raised in sharp form the problem of the relation between church and culture, while various 'liberation' theologies have seemed to suggest that the Kingdom of God could be achieved as an earthly reality.

2   These issues were not and are not peculiar to Anglicanism; but in many parts of the Communion they have come into particularly sharp focus. Anglican Christianity often arrived – in the Caribbean, for example, and in Africa, Asia, and the Pacific – in the wake of, or in close association with, British colonial administration. Its identity has thus inevitably been seen as closely tied to British culture, and its strengths and weaknesses have been understood in terms of the strengths and weaknesses of that culture. Particularly in the decades since the Second World War, there has been a natural and often harsh reaction against the colonial legacy; and one consequence of this reaction has been questioning or rejection of a Christianity heavily marked by its alien context, and apparently identified with the civilization of a colonizing power. The fact of this reaction has been an obstinately inescapable datum for our Commission: it quickly became clear to us that to be 'Anglican' not only *could* no longer be, but in fact *was* no longer, a matter of being 'English'.

3   The Anglican Consultative Council's appointment of a theological commission to look at these questions under the rubric of 'Church and Kingdom' reflects an insight of some importance. In so far as there has been a classical 'theory' about the nature of Anglicanism it has been closely connected with specific moments in the history of England: it has rested on the vision of a certain symbiosis of church and nation. Accordingly, when Anglicanism ceased to be the preserve of one nation and even of one realm (there is more than one nation in Britain), and gradually became a Christian family dispersed over the globe, it did so, on the whole, without a theology of its own identity independent of the English crown and the English law, and it has only developed such a theology in a somewhat piecemeal fashion. Anglicanism is often rebuked (not always justly) for having only a confused doctrine of the church; and it is true that one of the things our present difficulties press upon us is the need for clarification in this area – for an Anglican account of the nature of the Christian community *in itself* (not just as a civilization at prayer). Such a clarification is a necessary first step towards a theology of Anglican identity.

4   Hence the Commission's task was defined as an exploration of the complex relations between the Gospel and social or cultural forms in the light of the central assertion of the Gospel itself – that the Kingdom of God is at hand; that what God wills to effect through the ministry, death, and resurrection of Jesus is a new realization of his rule in the hearts and lives of human beings. The Kingdom is promised, then, but (as it has been put) what happens is the church. Every Christian theologian thus has the job of striving to understand the unity and the distinction of church and Kingdom. So our examination of Gospel and culture, church and context, has had to return constantly to the question of the meaning of that promised kingdom.

Given the terms of this assignment, we have not sought to deal directly or explicitly with the question of Anglican identity – though we suspect that this Report can serve to illustrate an Anglican perspective on the problems with which it deals. We are also aware that we have said almost nothing about those questions affecting the *internal* structure of the church that have so often preoccupied Anglican writers (the nature of episcopacy, for instance). In a report of limited length, we have been obliged to concentrate our attention on what we believe to be the necessary preconditions of more detailed work on such questions as these. There is still – and always will be – much more to be done.

The Commission's Own Experience

5   In our theological work we have made certain assumptions about how to proceed. The Commission has itself embodied the tensions it was formed to investigate; its members have come from widely divergent backgrounds, with different experiences and consequently with different ideas of Christian priorities. We have not been free to assume that any one starting-point was obvious, or that any one method was the natural one to follow. In the event, we have written out of the conviction that the concrete experience of particular Christians in particular localities does indeed, as is often claimed, possess theological significance: that is to say, the meaning of God's promise of his Kingdom is empty apart from some grasp of why it is good news *here* and *now*, and of those events and processes which are seen as embodying and pointing to the Kingdom in this or that bit of actual human history.

6   Thus we recognize that this document is – like all theological reflection – provisional; the history of good

theology is a story of constant renewal in fresh circumstances. And we recognize too that there is a certain irony in the character of the Report. While we affirm the multi-cultural, multi-lingual nature of Anglican Christianity, we compose our report in English. While we insist on the need for a theology rooted in the particular, we produce a consensus document, inevitably full of generalities. Even these ironies, however, call attention to two affirmations which, in the light of our experience together, we confidently make: that theological variety – even theological tension – can enrich our understanding of God's truth; and that we have found ourselves able to live with this variety, to pray within it, and to discover through it that we do not lack a common language of faith, hope, and love. The pages following exhibit the skeleton of this common language.

7   The fact that we have, as a Commission, grown together and felt ourselves deeply enriched by one another is evidenced by the very existence of this Report. Yet we know that the highly specialized 'community' of a team of theologians (however diverse their backgrounds) in regular personal contact is not easily translated into relations of larger bodies to each other. It is well known how true this can be in ecumenical dialogue! The closer people get to each other in the work of a commission, the less 'representative', in one sense, they become of their diverse constituencies. But this too has a positive side. The experience of our work together shows that theological variety need not mean a co-existence of sullenly non-communicating, self-sufficient worlds of discourse. Encounters change people and their systems: we may not want, at the end of the day, to change our initial priorities, but we shall at least see their fuller context and implications, and be made newly aware of common roots for diverse aspirations. Mutual probing and criticism can, in this

light, be anything but destructive, although it will not be painless – as, once again, we have discovered.

Some Warnings

8   There are three warnings that we should give. One is that we cannot and do not set out to resolve all the specific and local issues which concern the churches of the Anglican Communion today. That remains, if we are right, the task of the local and regional churches to whom we write, with their specific struggles, achievements, frustrations, and celebrations. We can only indicate the wider considerations of principle that a Christian community in a particular place might bring to its reflections and its planning.

9   It is important, in the second place, that this report be read as a whole: often, especially in our earlier sections, we have primarily been interested in raising questions, and indicating, as candidly as possible, some of the problems we ourselves confronted quite starkly and specifically in our earlier meetings as a Commission. We do not, by listing such matters, intend to foreclose conclusions or to weight the argument, but simply to report what our own initial conversations so rapidly brought to light.

10   A third warning is also in order. We have written of finding a 'common language'. Some readers may object to the imprecision of the language we use, some to our use of, or allusion to, what they think of as mere slogans; some to our lack of reference to the language of what they may regard as 'classical' theological, ecclesiastical, or ecumenical texts, ancient *and* modern. It needs to be said again that we have tried not to assume the absolute priority of any one traditional

style or 'canon' beyond the Bible, the ecumenical creeds, and the basic structures of our sacramental life. What we have searched for is a language that does not speak only to and for those familiar with the 'classical' voices of Augustine, Aquinas, Hooker, Barth, and so on, or only to and for those habituated to the conventions of contemporary ecumenical dialogue. Of course we have not been able to avoid phraseology that will sound controversial or even partisan to some; but necessarily abbreviated and condensed formulae may be the only way of marking out common ground in an enterprise like that of this Commission. And what in one person's ears may be a wearisome or unintelligible cliché ('liberation' is an often quoted example) will be a word or phrase representing matters of life or death to others.

11   Verbal fastidiousness can be an effective defence against the challenges and difficulties of listening. On this Commission we have all had to learn our way out of instant, confident, and dismissive reactions to each other's language. Our plea in this report for real mutual attention in the presence of scriptural revelation arises directly from our life as a group. In entering this caution against an easy reading of this report, a reading without imagination and self-questioning, we hope to open to the reader some possibility of sharing in a process for which all of us are profoundly grateful, and which this report intends not only to summarize but to celebrate.

2 Identifying Questions

12   The Inter-Anglican Theological and Doctrinal Commission first met in 1981 at Woking, just south-west of London, England. To many of us as we arrived, our assignment looked both a little vague and even perhaps a little dull. We had been instructed, by the Anglican Consultative Council, to take up the problem of the relation between the church and the Kingdom of God in the light of the doctrines of creation and redemption. As it turned out, however, the assignment was anything but dull, and not so much vague as it was rich and complex. No sooner had we introduced ourselves and begun to talk than we realized that this broad and apparently abstract issue focused a number of burning, difficult, and very concrete problems. This discovery came about as members of the Commission attempted, in their opening sessions, to explain to one another what this issue of church and Kingdom meant – practically and immediately – to them and to the churches they represented.

13   In the course of that initial exchange, it quickly dawned on all of us that our several situations were in many respects very different from one another; and this fact was reflected in the different issues that were foremost in our minds as we considered the question of church and Kingdom. For some of us the central problem was that of the cultural strangeness of Anglicanism – and indeed of Christianity – in a society with strong and mature religious traditions of its own. For others the primary problem was that of the 'establishment' style of Anglican theology and practice in settings where the burning issue was that of the economic and political oppression and degradation of the great majority of the population. For yet others it was the issue of the disengagement of the church from a culture and a social order with which it had become all

10

too thoroughly identified. These different perceptions of the church's situation – all of them corresponding to experienced realities – were accompanied, moreover, by different theological approaches, which had only this in common, that they were, to one degree or another, dissatisfied with characteristic Anglican stances on a wide range of issues having to do with the relation of church and society.

14   What these differences, and the conflicts which naturally accompanied them, made clear to all of us was the importance and centrality of the problem we had been set. What is meant by the rule, or kingship, or Kingdom of God? Where and how is it manifested? Can the saving presence of God – and so the presence of his Kingdom – be discerned in the insights and teachings of non-Christian cultures with the religious traditions or ways of life which they embody? Can the Kingdom be identified in social and political movements which arise without reference to the church and sometimes in conflict with it? And then too – whatever replies one might give to this set of questions – what is the role of the church itself in relation to God's Kingdom? Does it in itself *embody* the Kingdom in such a way that we can say the new creation is actually present in the church now? Or would it be better to speak of the church as a *sign* of the Kingdom, pointing to it, directing and urging us toward it? Or again is the distinction between embodiment and sign in fact a misleading one in this context? These questions bear directly on the proclamation of the Gospel of the Kingdom today – and not least because they raise the issue of the degree to which the Gospel can be adapted to *any* culture or historical movement (not excluding those that like to think of themselves as Christian) without surrendering its distinctive content.

15   Here, then, was a wide range of searching questions,

generated out of the problems which actually face the churches of the Anglican Communion today. As our discussions continued, however, it became apparent that there were other, perhaps even more fundamental, issues which had to be taken up if these questions were to be addressed constructively. How, for example, could Christians discuss *either* church *or* Kingdom without acknowledging that the meaning of both is determined by Jesus Christ in his ministry, death, and resurrection and in his coming as judge and deliverer? For if Christians as 'church' do in fact have a relation to God and God's Kingdom, that relation is constituted by God in Christ and through Christ, who is thus the central reality for Christian faith and thinking. Further, we were reminded that both the Gospel of the Kingdom – the good news which is Christ himself – and therefore the mission of the church assume that human life and history have somehow gone systematically wrong, and that this wrongness has consistently been understood in Christian tradition to be rooted in that perversion of human choice and love which we call 'sin' – not in creatureliness as such, not in chance or fate, but in the historical sphere of rational beings acting in liberty. To understand, then, the practical meaning of God's Kingdom, or of the church's relation to the world, account would have to be taken not only of creation and redemption, but also of the evil which spoils and denies the one and is healed by the other.

16   Finally, and by no means least in importance, there arose the issue *how and on what basis* Christians go about answering questions of the sort we were posing. No doubt it is easy – and correct – to say that God's self-disclosure in Christ is the central point of reference for Christians as they seek to understand God, themselves, and their world. But how is this self-disclosure mediated to us? How does it become a revelation

in which God's Kingdom grasps us and becomes real for us? Anglicans have always pointed to the Scriptures when confronted with this question, and then, secondarily, to the ecumenical creeds and other traditional expressions of the new life which God discloses and confers in Christ. None of these witnesses, however, speaks in a vacuum. They not only speak *out of* a particular historical situation, with its own problems and ways of thinking. They also speak *to* such a setting, to minds already formed, e.g., by culture or by the interests of a social class or a profession; by accepted notions of what is or is not likely to be true; and by forms of personal, political, or social commitment. Is it possible, then, that such factors – the mental spectacles through which believers read and understand the Scriptures and the deliverances of tradition – can themselves mediate God's self-disclosure? Thus the question of scriptural and traditional authority at once involved us in reflections on problems about interpretation and the norms of interpretation in various actual situations; and this led us back by another route to the questions with which we began – the questions of the church's relations to culture and history and to the various forms of struggle for personal, social, and political renewal or liberation.

17   In addressing these issues in this report, the Commission does not intend to provide – or to be seen as providing – final or definitive answers. The reasons for this should be obvious. For one thing, the members of the Commission are not themselves in agreement on all the questions which have been raised, and it would be dishonest to pretend otherwise. More important, however, is another consideration. The practical and theoretical problems which have been created for the churches of Christ by the cultural, political, and intellectual changes of the latter part of the twentieth century cannot be solved ahead of time on paper. The disagreements, debates,

and inquiries which accompany these changes are part of a process in which churches are seeking, in relatively novel circumstances, to reaffirm and reappropriate their identity and mission. In such a situation, there are of course many common affirmations which can be made, and there is much which can be said both to clarify issues and to exclude misunderstanding or one-sided solutions. The process of discovery itself, however, cannot be interrupted, for the way to the truth lies through it. This report, therefore, is an interim assessment of the situation. It aims, of course, to record agreements, but also to measure and map problems and help churches and their leaders to set their own concerns and preoccupations in wider context.

3 Belonging and not Belonging

18   We start, then, with the fact of the Anglican Communion, which represents one stream of tradition in the life of the universal people of God. Throughout the world, individual dioceses are united within themselves through the ministry of their bishops and pastors. They are joined to one another regionally in organized provinces and national churches. They share the heritage of post-Reformation English Christianity – a heritage which encompasses the tradition of the ancient and medieval churches but also includes its own theological style and agenda as well as its own ways of worship and pastoral administration.

19   If these churches belong to one another, however, and to a particular tradition within the church universal, they also belong to the places where their life is conducted and their work carried out. Each is set in a particular cultural world, which, although it is not static and continues to grow and be modified by its encounter with other cultures and experiences, has an identifiable style or idiom of its own. These cultural worlds differ – in the traditions and values they live by, in the habits of thought and behaviour they encourage. They differ not only from one another, but also from the world of Christian experience and tradition which is carried by Anglicanism. Even in England, where one would expect Anglicanism to be automatically 'at home', churches increasingly recognize that they represent something which in fact is relatively marginal to their cultural setting. To be sure, in England as elsewhere, our churches 'belong' to their settings. Their members, people and clergy alike, are shaped by the customs and beliefs which prevail in the world of their daily life. Hence they are naturally disposed to see, express, and exploit the continuities between those customs and

beliefs on the one hand and their Christian faith and life on the other. Nevertheless, they also discover obstacles and discontinuities which make complete assimilation to local culture both difficult and problematic. Wherever they exist, churches both belong and do not belong to the cultural world which is their immediate setting.

20   But it is not only a cultural world which is the setting of any particular church. It is also a social and political milieu. Wherever Christianity takes root, it builds itself, in one way or another, consciously or unconsciously, into an established structure of political and economic power. It makes institutional and social space for itself within the system which, in a given place and time, orders the distribution of wealth, privilege, and influence – and may indeed be, or become, partly responsible for the shape which that system takes. In doing so, it is, from one point of view, taking the steps necessary to assure its continued existence in an organized form. No community or institution can exist or function for long in despite of the constitutional, legal and economic systems which prevail in a given place. From another point of view, however, this means that churches can become involved with social and political systems that rest on a foundation of manifest injustice and oppression, and may even openly endorse such systems.

21   Anglicanism itself is a case in point. In England the legal establishment of the Church of England in the post-Reformation period intensified the close relationship that already existed between the church and the civil authorities. When Anglicanism went abroad in the colonial period, this involvement of church and state persisted, though in varying forms, with two kinds of consequences.

22   On the one hand, the church used its alliance with civil authority to promote Christian ideals and enhance human dignity. Educational and medical facilities were provided for colonized peoples, and in many places the groundwork was laid for the eventual attainment of national independence. On the other hand, missionaries and colonial administrators alike were, even at their best, deeply paternalistic. However good their intentions, they were inclined to treat the local people as children who in their eyes never grew up. Well-meant missionary slogans like 'the Bible and the Plough' or 'Christianity, Commerce, and Civilization' were all too easily corrupted to justify economic exploitation and the dominance of English culture. In this way the church became an unthinking accessory to economic exploitation and political servitude.

23   Thus the close relationship between Anglicanism and the civil administration of colonial territories was inherently ambivalent. It allowed scope for the church's social and moral witness, but at the same time it blunted the critical, prophetic edge of that witness. The point is, however, that this ambivalence admirably illustrates a perpetual tension in the church's life. A church belongs and yet does not belong to the social and political system under which it operates. Its life is both continuous and – even if sometimes only implicitly and in principle – discontinuous with the structures of its society.

24   Whether one thinks in cultural or in social-political terms, therefore, Christian churches – and so Anglican churches – live in a situation of tension. They belong and they do not belong; they are at once natives of their places and foreigners in it, at once lovers and affirmers of its life and critics of its ways. Normally, no doubt, this tension exists in a subdued and even suppressed form. Christians, like other folk, prefer to think that things are fundamentally all right;

they prefer to stick with what is familiar. Sticking with what is familiar, however, can sometimes result in moral and theological blindness. It can induce believers to miss points of conflict and discontinuity, where the churches have a critical – and necessarily also a *self*-critical – witness to bear on behalf of truth, righteousness, or justice. For this reason, the tension which is built into Christian existence must be admitted, explored, and understood. We have to ask why and how it is that Christians, as we have put it, belong and do not belong, and what this tension means – or ought to mean – in day-to-day practice of the faith.

4 Church and Kingdom in the Order of Redemption

25 Here is where our assigned questions about the church, the Kingdom of God, and their relation becomes directly relevant to the practical problems of the Anglican churches in their different cultures and societies. The tension between belonging and not belonging, between affirmation and criticism, which accompanies Christian existence does not stem from some regrettable or accidental circumstance. It is built into the very meaning of the word 'church', as a moment's reflection will show.

26 It is easy enough to say in general terms what the word 'church' refers to. It denotes certain organized human communities or assemblies, taken either individually or collectively. If, however, one wants a notion of what these groups mean by calling themselves 'church', then it is necessary to observe what they say about themselves in the common actions – that is, the liturgies – in which they characteristically engage when gathered. In these liturgies, they read and expound sacred books; they offer prayer and praise; they initiate members by a ritual of washing; they solemnly celebrate a sacred meal. Further, in each of these actions they refer their shared life to a transcendent source which is named 'God' and 'Christ' and 'Spirit'; and they testify that this transcendent reality to which their actions point is experienced as redemptive – as at once liberating and fulfilling.

27 If, though, they are asked to locate or characterize this redemptive reality more narrowly, Christians will point in the first instance to Jesus the Christ, the crucified, risen, and expected Lord. He is the church's foundation, the principle of

its life, the one in whom, through the Spirit, it has access to God. The existence of this phenomenon called 'church' does not revolve primarily around a creed, or a set of doctrines, or an ethical programme, but around Christ himself, whose meaning for human existence creeds, doctrines, and ethical prescriptions attest and explain. A particular group is called 'church', then, because its members have met and know a good – a grace – that touches their experience even though it is beyond them. This good thing both evokes their repentance and brings forgiveness, and they claim it for themselves by accepting a call to fellowship with Jesus Christ – a call to be his disciples, to share in his life, and to be, as St. Paul put it, 'in Christ'. This does not mean that such persons are a spiritual and moral élite; for their fellowship with Christ and in Christ is that of disciples and forgiven sinners – beginners upon a way. It does mean, however, that their common life in all its dimensions signifies Christ. He is what the church stands for.

28   What Jesus the Christ stood for and stands for, however, is the Kingdom of God. The Gospels make it plain that the theme and promise of Jesus' ministry, the redemptive reality which he proclaimed, was the *basileia tou theou*, the 'reign' or 'kingship' or 'Kingdom' of God. They also make it plain that the relationship between Jesus' ministry and this Kingdom was a very special one. The aim of Jesus' ministry was not to build or create that Kingdom by carrying out some sort of plan or programme. Rather, his mission was to announce and signify it – to open people's eyes to the fact that God was with them in a new way for grace and for judgement.

29   In his preaching, teaching, and healing, therefore, Jesus brought the reality of God's 'new thing' home to people: he gave them a taste of what his ministry promised. What it

promised was the putting of the world to right – the fulfilment of all the good things that had been foreshadowed both in the proclamation of the prophets and in the history of Israel. His ministry promised the actualization of God's righteous will, and so the defeat of evil and the triumph of justice and goodness. It promised fellowship with God and all his redeemed people, and the knowledge of God 'face to face'. Jesus' ministry promised these things, moreover, not for individuals taken in isolation, but for persons in community. Implicitly, therefore, it pointed to a new life in the shape of a new social order, a new style of life together. This promise of redemption, manifested in signs, and attested by the 'righteousness, peace, and joy in the Holy Spirit' (Rom. 14.17) experienced in the Christian community, would be fully realized in the restoration of all things at the coming of Jesus in power and glory, when the whole creation would be transformed.

30 At the same time, Jesus' ministry aimed at evoking a particular response to the promise of God's Kingdom. This promise was the one thing worth living for, the 'one pearl of great value', for whose sake the merchant 'went and sold all that he had' (Matt. 13.46). Hence, of people who were confronted with the good news of the Kingdom, Jesus required repentance, 'change of mind'. That is, he did not demand merely that they mend their ways, but that they change their style of acting and living by changing the whole way in which they saw, estimated, and valued things. They were to set their hearts primarily on God's reign and God's justice, and care for that more than they cared for 'getting on' in the world. What is more, Jesus exemplified the 'change of mind' that he preached. He surrendered his life out of trust in God and in God's promise and out of fidelity to God's will. He became a victim – even a fool – for the sake of God's Kingdom.

21

31 In the end, therefore, there is no way of understanding the role of Jesus in relation to the kingship of God without taking account of his death and resurrection. He was executed at the hands of the Roman authorities and raised to a new life with God; and these are not just interesting or astonishing circumstances, but the events in and through which his manifestation of God's reign was accomplished. The rejection and death of Jesus are a measure of the alienation which divine love and the human repentance it evokes must overcome. There is a gulf – a gulf which is concretely symbolized in the violent rejection and killing of Jesus by those for whom he came – between the world as human beings have made it and that same world transformed as God's Kingdom. Jesus' self-surrender in death – his walking with us and with us in the path of repentance – marks the way to God's new creation. Further, the fact that the one who thus gave himself up was vindicated by God in the resurrection means that the promise of his ministry, the promise of God's reign, was no deception. It has been fulfilled in his own person. He has been revealed, in his own person, as the very 'grace and truth' which he had conveyed by word and deed – as the one in whom and through whom God's reign is realized.

32 In the light of the resurrection, then, the world of human life takes on a new aspect. It can now be seen to have the Kingdom of God – that divine reign which has 'come true' in Christ and can even now be tasted and experienced in the Spirit – as the reality that frames it, and thus gives it meaning and defines its destiny. The world, we might say, has the Kingdom of God as its 'horizon'. Yet, as this metaphor suggests, the resurrection does not abolish the distance between God's Kingdom and the world as human beings have made it. What God has in store for those who love him still

lies on the other side of repentance, self-surrender to God and death to individual and corporate egotism with its fearful refusal of love. The Kingdom of God is indeed the world's horizon, but at the same time its *transcendent* horizon. It is not something which is simply given in the common sense, every-day world of unchallenged untransformed perceptions. 'Do you not know that all of us who have been baptized into Jesus Christ were baptized into his death? We were buried therefore with him by baptism into death, so that as Christ was raised from the dead by the glory of the Father, we too might walk in newness of life' (Rom. 6.3–4). This new life is lived not only by faith but in hope. We may not know what the reign of God will be like when fully come, but we are led to link it with the revealing of God's Son from heaven and the resurrection of the dead. The baptized Christian receives the Spirit as a pledge of the day when this mortal body will be changed to be like Christ's already glorious body.

33 When we talk about the church, therefore, and say that it has Christ as its foundation, or that it lives 'in Christ', or that it stands for Christ, this in the end is no different from saying that the church refers itself to, and has as its principle in the strictest sense, the Kingdom of God. As a body of disciples and beginners, taken on by grace and forgiveness, the church touches and experiences the beginnings of the 'new thing' which God is doing – and does so because, in Christ, this 'new thing' is already accomplished. Further, the church, as a body of disciples, is engaged in the same business as its Lord: that of opening the world to its horizon, to its destiny as God's Kingdom. Not only by proclamation but also by deed, the church is called to let God's Kingdom show in the world and for the world – to give the world a taste, an inkling, of 'the glory which shall be revealed'. Finally – and again as a body of disciples – the church follows the way of repentance,

because that is the way along which God's Kingdom is found. While baptism signifies repentance for the remission of sins – a radical conversion from darkness to light and the beginning of a new life – those who follow Christ have nevertheless to repent and to take up the cross daily. To be 'church' is always to be turning to God, always to be in transition to a better mind, always to be answering afresh the call of God in Christ as events and circumstances make that call concrete. When Christians assemble as the church of God for worship they lift up their hearts to Christ as the Lord who already has received all authority in God's Kingdom and who is awaiting the final overcoming of opposition to his reign. This tasting of the powers of the age to come, by sharing in the Holy Spirit (Heb. 6.4–5), inspires the church with the hope of glory but also brings it constantly under the judgement of Christ's rule and authority. Christ comes as judge; he stands at the door and knocks and comes in to sup with those who hear his voice and open the door.

34 It is important not to terminate this thinking about the church merely on the assembly at worship or on a diocesan or provincial body. We have spoken of the church as 'a body of disciples'. These disciples are usually to be found dispersed in their communities as (from one point of view) 'aliens and exiles' (1 Pet. 2.11) and it is in their various vocations and in the business of their ordinary lives and in their engagement with their neighbours that the world is made aware of its destiny as God's Kingdom. When ordinary Christians act in the world they exercise what a recent ecumenical document calls 'Christian authority' by which 'men perceive the authoritative word of Christ' (ARCIC *Final Report*, Authority I, 3, p. 53). Often, indeed, Christians act collectively in their work and witness; for the most part, however, they appear not as members of the church but as persons having roles and

tasks in society. In the latter capacity they make decisions and respond to events that make the call of God in Christ concrete, and thus become the occasion of repentance and of the active witness to which it leads. There is ambiguity in this, for all do not respond in the same way to what the occasion may seem to require. Nevertheless, the effective witness of God's people to the presence and coming of the Kingdom of God resides more in the meaning and quality of their lives than it does in the decisions and acts of church councils.

35 But if all this is true, it is not hard to identify the ultimate source of that tension in which Christians and Christian churches live with the world around them. On the one hand, the Kingdom of God which is revealed and established in Christ affirms the world as God's. The world is the subject of redemption and so the object of God's love. There is continuity between its present life and its fulfilment in Christ. On the other hand, the Kingdom of God which is established and revealed in Christ stands to this same world as 'beyond' – a transcendent hope – and therefore questions and relativizes it. Thus the crucified and risen Lord embodies a redemption which at once affirms the world and judges it; and the church, a segment of its world, lives uneasily on the borderline between belonging and not belonging.

5 World and Kingdom in the Order of Creation

36 The Christian experience of redemption, however – which is the experience of God's Kingdom in Christ – has implications which go beyond questions about the life and mission of the church. It also has something to say about the world itself and about the world's relation to God's Kingdom. When St. Paul describes the saving work of Christ as new creation (2 Cor. 5.17), his very language intimates the understanding of the world which the Gospel presupposes. His words are rooted in what in his day was already an established tradition regarding creation and fall, and it is this tradition which tells us in effect what sort of world it is for which redemption in Christ is both possible and necessary.

37 The doctrine of creation – developed over many generations by Jewish and Christian exegetes – is based not only on the opening chapters of Genesis but on a whole series of scriptural passages, some of the most prominent of which are in the Psalms and Isaiah 40–55. What these passages envisage is a divine act of creation that embraces 'all things visible and invisible' – the whole of the natural order and humanity within it. The teaching which they set out is neither an alternative to, nor a substitute for, scientific accounts of the structure and history of the natural order. What science studies is the world which we inhabit in all its immensity and richness. The doctrine of creation, on the other hand, affirms that this same world owes its very being to God and belongs to God. Destined from the beginning to be God's Kingdom, to be transparent to his loving will, the world subsists through God's Word and in God's Spirit, having been brought into existence 'out of nothing'. Hence creatures are, and become themselves most perfectly, not apart from God but in openness to God – even as God manifests his being as love by

calling the world into existence, caring for it, and sustaining it. What the doctrine of creation sets forth, then, is the fact that the world is *for* God precisely because, at the same time, God is *for* the world. Thus the whole of the universe – this visible physical and material universe – is God's creation, which can and does 'declare the glory of God' (Psalm 19.1).

38 In the Genesis stories of creation, a special place is assigned to the making of humanity, which is presented as the climax of God's creative undertaking. The first of these stories dignifies 'Adam', male and female, as the creature made after God's 'image and likeness' (Gen. 1.26–27). The second shows God moulding the first human out of the earth, breathing life into this creature, and finally settling him and his companion in a Garden to live off the bounty of God. Closely examined, these stories carry a wealth of meaning at many levels. As God's 'image', Adam is set over the other creatures of God and thus given a calling under God to foster and continue the work of creation. Here the human being is portrayed in a way that portends all its creative activities – as farmer, technologist, artist, scientist. But Adam's fellowship in the second story is not only with the creatures of other species, animate and inanimate; he is given a companion, another of his own kind, with whom to share life. And here humanity is symbolically portrayed in its essentially social character – as the bringer to birth of families, nations, and cultures. As the image and likeness of God, then, this Adam is created to be 'with' an 'other', to be one who communicates, shares, and co-operates – a creature whose life is tied up in language in the most inclusive sense of that term. And as such, of course, this human being is an 'answerable' creature, one that exercises freedom in its calling under God to be accountable to others and for others and in this way to reflect and manifest the creative love and power of God.

39 In all this, one theme is very clear. The stories of creation are an affirmation of the world, not just as something which is 'very good' in itself, but even as something which, because it is *for God*, is in principle holy. Despite the groaning and travailing of creation, people who have faith see that the world, including humanity, reflects God and by its very being praises and points to God. Conversely, God is never unmindful of or absent from the world. God is present for it as the context and horizon of its being, providing, ruling, and overruling for the sake of the fulfilment which Christ brings and embodies – the day which will mean that God is 'everything to every one' (1 Cor. 15.28).

40 No sooner is this said, however, than it is necessary to recall that the stories in Genesis about the origins of things turn immediately from the narrative of creation to that of the fall. The first thing to be said about the world is that it is God's work and the sphere of God's kingship –that the very logic of its being points to God not merely as the source but as the completer and fulfiller of its life. But almost before this witness of faith has been completed, a second proposition is added: God's world is spoiled, alienated from him, and handed over to bondage. Alongside the mystery of creation is set the mystery of sin. Humanity – Adam – rebels against God, against the source and archetype of its own being.

41 The story of Adam's fall has figured largely in Christian tradition – and rightly so. Certain Christians may often regret and criticize speculations to which the story has given rise – speculations, for example, about the way in which sin is inherited or contracted. What they cannot question, however, is that the story of the fall intends to tell people something about themselves – not just as individuals but collectively – and that what it has to say rings true. 'Adam'

means 'humanity'; and – as St Paul would have put it – we (not just 'I') are *in Adam* – caught together with the rest of our race in a state or condition of sin which feeds on itself. What is more, the evil which this story contemplates is not rightly understood simply as an affliction of helpless humanity by hostile non-human forces, or as a matter of mere limitation or ignorance. Whatever role in the origins of our fallen state may have been ascribed to Satan, Christian theology has consistently claimed that the sin in which humanity is 'tied and bound' is grounded in human choosing. That choosing may be shaped by factors which are as much social and historical as they are individual. Sin is not re-invented by each successive person who is born into the world. It belongs to the structures of human life together, as well as being personal and individual. Nevertheless the story of Adam's fall is right when it locates ultimate responsibility for moral evil in the human act of choice. Even though there seems to be a tragic inevitability about moral evil, its root must be sought in the perversion of human willing and loving. The Creator made human beings to be with one another and with God; 'Adam', however, wants autonomy – not the freedom which is born of love, but the freedom which consists of being 'in-dependent', not beholden, self-sufficient. Such freedom, however, is in the end self-defeating and self-destructive. And that is the heritage of the 'first Adam': God's creation spoiled.

42 Nor is this insistence on human fallenness a matter merely of abstract doctrine. To moderns who, to one extent or another, enjoy the benefits of the revolution of communications, the evidence of human evil is great enough to be almost numbing to the will. People do not merely become accustomed to the sorts of evil which are done and suffered in individual and familial relationships. More and more they are aware of the social and collective dimensions of sin and of the

self-righteous zeal with which hatred, moral indifference, the oppression of one group or class by another, the wastage of the earth's resources, the escalation of the arms race, and the active violence of nation against nation are justified and even glorified. In the face of these realities, people tend naturally either to look for scapegoats on whom the problems can be blamed or else to take refuge in cynical resignation. But no one, if the story of Adam contains the truth which Christians have found in it, can pretend to be uninvolved in human sinning. The evil in which humanity is caught cannot be distanced by projecting it on others or by claiming tacitly to be above it all. No one is personally and individually responsible for all – or even for much – of the evil which the world contains; but neither does any one stand apart from it. It is not only this person or that who has gone wrong, but Adam; and Adam's capacity to get things wrong seems to increase with human power and ingenuity.

43 A Christian appreciation of the world as creation, then, states the presuppositions of the message of redemption in Christ. The world is God's creation. As such, it is good. Both the natural order and the world of history – of human decision and action – have their ground and their end in God, who is present in them and for them to finish his creative work. Yet this same world – secondarily but not less truly – is spoiled, nor is any person, group of persons, or realm of activity exempt from the effects of the systemic perversion of choosing and loving. Thus God's Kingdom is native to the human world and foreign to it: native by God's creation and providence, foreign by human sin. The tension between grace and judgement, affirmation and criticism, is present not merely in the message of the New Testament but throughout the Scriptures.

6 God's Kingdom: A Yes and a No

44 It is this tension which provides the framework within which Anglican churches can appreciate and weigh the issues – about the relation of church and culture or about the relation of church and political order – which now confront them.

45 The genesis of these problems in their contemporary form is familiar to everyone. The spread of Christianity in the modern era was one aspect of a general expansion of the power and the influence of the nations and peoples of western Europe. This colonialist movement did not always take the form of literal colonization, but it invariably led – in spite of real humanitarian achievements – to the economic, political, and cultural subjection of local populations. At the same time, it helped to bring about a world order in which, as never before, peoples in many parts of the world find themselves inter-related parts of a single economic and political 'scene'. What in the final analysis enabled these developments was the industrial and the technological revolution which accompanied the era of colonial expansion. These revolutions have made increasingly swift travel and communication possible between widely distant parts of the earth. They have transformed the economy of nation after nation, in every section of the globe. Most important of all, perhaps, it is they – and the values and ideas they generate – which have come to define the common cultural milieu of the contemporary world.

46 Today, however, with the disappearance of traditional colonial empires (though not the world which they helped create), formerly subject peoples are rediscovering and reasserting their own political, economic, and cultural integrity. They seek, both at a domestic and an international level, to

reverse the political and economic injustices which in part are the legacy of the colonial era.* By the same token, they seek to reaffirm their cultural identities – to reappropriate, where necessary, the customs, values, and insights that belong to their local or regional ways of life. To be sure, these efforts do not, and cannot, contemplate a return to the state of affairs which prevailed before the beginnings of the centuries-long colonial era. The possibility of a relatively isolated existence for any people or culture has become almost inconceivable. Already we live in a world in which, quite apart from considerations of economic interdependence, there is a lively interchange of political and religious ideas, as well as of styles of art, dress, and life. The setting of these efforts to achieve integrity and justice is a global and international one to begin with, and the issues therefore concern peoples everywhere.

47 They also concern the Anglican churches, which first became a world-wide communion, and only later discovered themselves as such, in the course of the movement of colonial expansion and its aftermath. Planted in North America, the Caribbean, Africa, Asia, and the lands of the Pacific, these churches still, to one degree or another, represent something of an English presence in a series of non-English environments. To be sure, if displaced 'Englishness' were the sole problem, its solution might best be left to time and changing circumstance. Where matters of language are concerned – or styles in art and architecture, or customs in the worship and pastoral administration of the churches – one would expect that the natural tendency of communities and institutions to

* Though political independence has now been attained in most countries of the 'South', their economies are, nevertheless, still appendages to the economies of the 'North', in whose favour the international economic order is heavily biased. See *Brandt Report*, Pan Books, London 1981.

adapt to their setting would gradually erode any intolerable foreignness. The truth is, however, that the problems go much deeper than this obvious problem of 'Englishness' and touch issues of theological substance.

48 The first such problem is that created by the struggle of peoples in the Third World for economic and political liberation. The experience of oppression and of the action and thought involved in overcoming it have become, in such settings, a matrix which reshapes both the life of the churches and the style of theological reflection which goes on in them. Not only is this the case, but it appears to Christians who are involved in this struggle that traditional forms of worship, of piety, and of theology are tied up with a social and economic system which is insensitive to the cry of the poor for justice and therefore resists significant social change. For such persons, it is the experience of oppression and struggle itself which provides the vantage-point from which the true meaning of Christian faith can be discerned; and this experience is therefore an occasion when God's presence and God's will are grasped.

49 A second such problem is that of the relation of Christianity and Christian theology in their traditional forms to the religious thought, symbols, and insights of non-Christian cultures. At bottom this is an issue about the validity of the forms of religious experience and practice embodied in such cultures; hence it requires, if it is to be addressed usefully, not so much a history as a theology of religions. Christians have to ask whether their faith is truly and ultimately 'foreign' in the setting of a cultural and religious tradition that has no relation to that of the Christian West, or whether, on the contrary, such a tradition may provide a source of illumination for Christians in their understanding

and communication of the Gospel of Christ – even while, at the same time, it is illumined and interpreted by that Gospel. Is there a revelation of God in the history and common experience of non-Christianized cultures?

50 Each of these issues, then, raises a challenge, not to Anglicanism particularly or specifically, but, more broadly, to long-standing western or European forms of Christian life and theology. These are perceived as alien to the experience of peoples whose life and sensibility are shaped primarily by the struggle against oppression and injustice, or by a cultural and religious tradition foreign to western and European ways of thought. Hence the question is raised whether, in such settings as these, Christian faith does not necessarily take new and indigenous forms, as indeed it did with the conversion of the peoples of western Europe. And if this is so, is it not reasonable to think that God has somehow truly spoken and bestowed himself through these modes of experience to illumine the meaning of the Gospel in a fresh way?

51 To raise this question and to deal with it soberly is not an easy thing. It is the sort of question which tends to evoke quick, unconsidered, and emotional responses from people on every side of it – not least because it requires everyone to step mentally outside of commitments and habits of mind which have become settled. On the other hand, there are some fairly clear principles which can help people to understand and discuss the question.

52 First of all, it is crucial to take note of the historical setting in which all these questions of ours are raised. Everything we have said hitherto has stressed the fact that historical – and therefore cultural and social – context is a central factor in people's understanding and appropriation of the Gospel of

Christ. If this is so, however, it is incumbent on us to acknowledge and identify the situation or setting that is presupposed by the questions we are addressing. And the most important thing to notice is the fact that these questions are not generated as issues specific to any particular culture. On the contrary, they arise out of the meeting and interaction of previously isolated traditions. Their setting, then, is from the start multi-cultural and international – a fact attested by the very composition of this Commission. Merely to raise them is to put oneself in a special and peculiar sort of situation: that of a person who both belongs and does not belong to his or her own specific setting as, say, African or English or Polynesian or North American. In other words, the questions themselves define a context in which every cultural or national setting is important, and none can be assumed to be intrinsically more important or less in question than any other.

53 In the second place, it is important to consider what it is that makes it possible for believers to come together in such a context: to speak as representatives of widely differing experiences and ways of life and yet as people who belong together. The explanation does not lie simply in our common Anglicanism. No more can it be sought simply in the fact that modern technology has created a common space for meeting. People's capacity to take such a stance depends on their acknowledgement of the universality of the redemption which Christ represents and carries and of which the church, through the Holy Spirit, has foretaste. What undergirds and supports such dialogue, in short, is the faith, grounded in the death and resurrection of Christ and confirmed through the gift of the Spirit, that the human world in all its variety is at once from God and for God: that its transcendent horizon is God's Kingdom.

54　In the light of that faith – which is the only light by which the church, as church, can judge anything – one positive affirmation is clearly required. That the message of God's redemption in Christ is truly addressed to every nation indicates that there is, in the life and history of every people, that which looks toward or opens itself to Christ. This can only mean, however, that in the historical experience of every people the Creator God provides, through that divine Word 'in whom all things consist', the basis on which the Kingdom can be recognized and appropriated. Whether one thinks of the experience of struggle for justice and peace, then, or of religious traditions and practices which mediate experience of the ultimate 'Other' as the horizon and goal of human existence, it is natural and right to see in them ways which God employs to be present with his people and to be known to them.

55　At this point, though, two other considerations come into play. First of all, when Christians make this judgement, they do so not from some vantage-point above time and history, but as people who know themselves and their destiny through God's gracious gift of himself in Christ. What they can affirm about the presence of God in the world's struggles for justice and for peace, or in the insights embodied in the traditions of other religions, they affirm not in spite of, but because of, their knowledge of God in Christ. It is the God who raised Jesus Christ from the dead, and therefore the justice and peace made known in God's at-one-ment of humanity in Christ, which for them remain regulative and whose traces or lineaments they are glad to discern and affirm wherever it is possible.

56　Then in the second place, just because, in the light of God's redemption in Christ, believers are aware of the reality of sin in their own individual and common lives, they know that it is at work in their world as well, spoiling God's creation and his gifts. They know that even the search for peace and justice can produce violence and oppression as its fruits, and that depth of religious insight – Christian and non-Christian alike – can be perverted to the service of falsehood.

57 To be sure, none of this means – or should be taken to mean – that God is not at work in the world, revealing himself and therefore known in the political and religious life of peoples everywhere. It does mean, however, that in all particular situations there are critical judgements to be made – serious judgements, but also judgements which must be nuanced, interrogative, provisional. And the question is how – on what basis and in what spirit – such judgements are to be made.

7 Pluralism and the Norms of Christian Judgement

58 What constitutes the ultimate basis of judgement for Christian believers is Christ himself. He is the one who represents and embodies the world's (and the church's) transcendent horizon, the Kingdom of God. The church is joined to Christ, however, and therefore knows Christ, through certain characteristic institutions and actions which mark and define its life. The English Reformers – in this agreeing with their contemporaries on the European continent – defined these as the preaching of the Word of God and the administration of the sacraments (Article 19). They further located the normative form of the Word of God in the Scriptures even while insisting that the baptismal rule of faith of the early church, the Apostles' and the Nicene creeds, attests and conveys the same central truth as the Scriptures. Proximately, therefore, and in practice, the basis on which the church speaks of Christ and makes its judgements is the set of institutions which mediate its relation to Christ: the Scriptures, the creeds, and – though in a different and complementary way – the sacramental life.

59 The Scriptures and creeds, however, must be interpreted reliably if they are to be understood and applied correctly. Thus the question arises in what light, by reference to what context or framework of understanding, they are to be interpreted. To this question, Anglicans have traditionally returned a twofold answer. The proper settings or contexts in which Scripture and creeds are understood are those supplied by tradition and reason.

60 By 'tradition', of course, one may mean the deposit of faith itself – the witness of the Scriptures and of the ancient

baptismal confession. For our purposes, however, it is a second sense of 'tradition' which is most important. In this sense, 'tradition' refers to the continuing life of the Christian community itself – the patterns of behaviour and habits of belief which are transmitted from generation to generation in the church. This tradition finds its primary, though by no means its sole, vehicle in the liturgies of the assembled community of believers. These provide a setting of symbolic word and action by which the Scriptures and creeds, as they are recited or explained, are illumined and enabled to 'speak'. To put the matter in other words, the church's liturgy carries the common mind of the community; and it is this 'mind', with its characteristic questions, interests, and assumptions, that receives, and in receiving interprets, the Bible and the creeds. Since, moreover, the 'mind' in question is one which has been formed over many generations by engagement with the very Scriptures and creeds it interprets for us, its testimony is a weighty one.

61 A second, and not less important, instrument of inter-pretation is what seventeenth-century Anglican teachers called 'reason'. Like 'tradition', this term has a wide range of meanings. Most fundamentally, perhaps, it signifies the native capacity of human persons to grasp and share the meanings of things through words and symbols. It also refers, more narrowly, to a particular manifestation of this capacity: the ability to think about things in consecutive, logical fashion. When understood and defined in this way, however, reason cannot be disentangled from the interpretative work of tradition, nor even from that of faith itself, since both of these involve the capacity to grasp and understand reality through the use of words and symbols.

62 In practice, however, the word 'reason' had a further

meaning as well. It referred not only to the mind's ability to grasp and handle ideas, but also to generally accepted notions of what fits or is 'reasonable' in the world as human beings see and experience it. Part, in other words, of what 'reason' meant was 'common sense' in the proper and serious sense of that phrase: not just a shared human capacity to think and understand, but a shared set of understandings and ideas. Defined in this way, reason was thought by seventeenth-century theologians to be independent of the specific norms and traditions of any Christian community, because it represented a heritage that belonged not to believers as such but to all human beings. Thus the importance of reason in the interpretation of Scriptures and creeds lay in the fact that as an instrument of understanding and criticism it was a gift of the Creator shared by Christians and non-Christians alike. It represented not the church's, but humanity's, 'common mind'.

63 In the present-day world, of course, thinkers are likely to take a somewhat different view of reason in its character as 'common sense'. They are vividly aware of the fact that what people take to be 'reasonable' tends to vary from time to time and from place to place. For them, therefore, what the seventeenth century called 'reason' is, in significant part, a matter of culture. It refers to the way of seeing things and asking about them which determines, for a given group of people in a given time and place, what 'makes sense', whether that group represents a critical minority or the majority in a particular society. Even when characterized in this way, though, reason is just as important a factor in the under-standing and interpretation of Christian faith as the seventeenth-century divines took it to be. It does indeed signify the common standards of judgement – about matters of fact and value alike – which believers share with non-believers, even though it can no longer be understood as a

universal norm but is more or less specific to a given society or culture. Reason too, then, as the common mind of a culture, works to influence what people will notice in the Scriptures and creeds, how they will seee them, what questions they will direct to them, and in general what sense they will make of them.

64 How, though, are we to assess the roles of tradition and reason? Anglicans, in the spirit both of the early church and of the Reformation, have always insisted that Scripture is the primary and sufficient norm of faith. They have also tended to translate this principle into a conviction that Scripture can be read and understood in absolute independence both of the church's tradition and of the 'reason' – the secular tradition, if you like – which a particular culture or society embodies. Yet it is not certain either that such a state of affairs is possible or that, if possible, it would be a desirable one.

65 The Scriptures and creeds are not, to be sure, infinitely malleable. They cannot be made out to say just anything at all. On the other hand, their speaking is always *in a setting*, and it is always in relation to what that setting regards as interesting and reasonable that they are heard to speak. Without context – in a vacuum, as it were – they would not be heard at all. The contexts afforded both by the mind of the church and by that of a broader culture, by tradition and by 'reason', are thus the primary sounding-boards of God's word.

66 Now it is true that these sounding-boards operate for the most part automatically and unconsciously. The interests, attitudes, values, and convictions which make them up are the set of common assumptions which provide the basis of a shared life, and as such they are seldom brought into focus themselves. Hence there is bound to be selectivity and

distortion about the way in which they make the Scriptures heard. For the most part the Scripture will be heard in a way which accords with the 'givens' – the world-view, the social ideology, the concerns and problems – of the society, culture, or sub-culture which hears them. A certain amount of selectivity and distortion is involved in the very act of translation from one language to another; for languages 'carry' cultural worlds. Yet – and this point needs stressing – such selectivity and distortion may well be a price that has to be paid for genuine insight into the Scriptures. The bias of a given tradition or point of view may bring to light truth which only it can serve to discern. In any case, such selectivity, and the distortion which may accompany it, are part of what is meant by bringing the message of the Scriptures 'home' to people; for home is the social and mental world in which they live.

67 Furthermore, in the process of understanding and interpreting the Scripture, there is a way in which selectivity and distortion can be – not finally or absolutely but significantly – corrected. For it happens, and not rarely, that there is conflict between what the Scriptures and creeds say in one context and what they say in another. The frequent dissonance between tradition and reason – between the 'sense' which Scripture makes in the life of the church and the 'sense' it makes in, say, a secularized culture – is one example of this. Another example might be the dissonance between the way Scripture is heard in a culture shaped by Islamic tradition and in one shaped by Hindu or Buddhist belief and practice; or that between the message it conveys to oppressed and marginalized groups and the message it conveys to dominant or comfortable groups in society. Such dissonances serve an interpretative purpose. They compel people to bring into focus the tradition and the reason, the common mind, in

the light of which they have been reading and understanding the Scriptures, and to let the Scriptures themselves challenge that mind in the face of another reading of them.

68 The Scriptures and the creeds never speak apart from a context, then; hence our understanding of them is always conditioned – by culture, by social structures and attitudes, by a given world-view. On the other hand, the Scriptures and the creeds speak in many contexts, both in the history of the church itself and in the various cultures and societies of the contemporary world; and it is this fact which, in the end, can set them free from the narrowing or distorting effects of any particular way of reading them. The pluralism of the world church – and of the Anglican Communion – creates problems for everyone. It requires everyone not merely to tolerate differences (which may, in the circumstances, be all too easy a course) but also to focus and to face the contextual factors which may have distorted or narrowed their own understanding of the Scriptures, the creeds, and so of the Christ whom these institutions mediate. But if pluralism and the dissonances which accompany it are sources of discomfort, they can also prompt and enable new insight and 'change of mind'.

69 To many people, this word 'pluralism' will be alarming. It may suggest *relativism*, the idea that there are no final criteria for what we say or do, and so no ultimate truth: that all we have are the conventions of the setting in which we happen to find ourselves. This is not what we mean by pluralism. In order to make our understanding of pluralism clear, however, it will be useful to differentiate three ways – each with disturbing implications – in which relativism is commonly understood.

(i) The most radical and general kind of relativism maintains that cultures and languages constitute, for all practical purposes, closed systems that are opaque to each other. There are no full and adequate translations from one human context to another. If this is the case, there can be no sense in talking about 'humanity' as a whole or about a common goal or destiny for human beings. Yet the Gospel carries a missionary mandate: it is proclaimed on the assumption that it is relevant to everyone of whatever race, class, culture, language, or religion.

(ii) Relativism can also be maintained in a more modest form. We may take it that in fact there is a common humanity and a common core of human experience, including what is identified as religious experience, but that the articulation of this experience differs from culture to cullture, so that no one expression of it can claim centrality or authority. Yet the Church claims that God has spoken and acted decisively in Jesus of Nazareth: other 'religious' utterances are judged by the Christian in the light of this belief.

(iii) More modestly still, relativism might be said to hold within the Christian community. Within the broad compass of a general commitment to the memory or inspiration of Jesus, many theological emphases are legitimate; and no doctrinal or credal statement can limit the possible plurality of Christian views. Yet the church has traditionally claimed and exercised the right to block off certain avenues of theological development, right up to the present time. (Several churches have recently declared the theological defence of apartheid to be heresy.)

70 Our own use of 'pluralism' does not represent any of these varieties of relativism. The *first* kind is, in fact, very difficult even to state intelligibly. Imperfect communication and translation do not imply totally sealed-off mental worlds. People of different cultures recognize each other as human beings, and, however difficult a foreign language or culture

may appear, they will enter into tentative conversations expecting to find a picture of human existence that has something in common with their own. A language that had no way of talking about being a body, being born, loving, coupling, dying would not be a human language at all. Our physical nature and our mortality provide the beginning of a common 'agenda', and it has yet to be shown that there could be *human* languages, in any worthwhile sense, with which we could not begin to engage on the basis of this kind of assumption.

71 But this extreme of relativism does remind us that we learn to know only within the limits of history and locality, speech and body. We cannot arrive at a universal standpoint, a theoretical account of our total situation. If the notion of a general or universal account of human nature emerges at all, it does so as a distant and elusive assumption on which people begin to operate *in* the process of encounter and conversation – that is to say, *in* the experience of human variety, not in an escape to some supra-human vantage point. As we shall see, this has implications for our view of the theological task.

72 The *second* kind of relativism raises more problems. On the one hand, we are bound to say that there can be no 'theology of religions' from a standpoint beyond all particular religious traditions: theology has to 'stand' somewhere, and to think otherwise is to betray an abstract and individualistic understanding of religion itself. The very idea of a 'religious experience' divorced from the life of specific religious communities is fraught with difficulties. On the other hand, people of differing traditions and commitments do talk with one another, and may recognize common ground; many faiths allow that their utterances about God have a provisional character, and some would see their systems as open to illumination from the experience of others.

73 This is a delicate and difficult area. To be a Christian at all is to be committed to acting on the assumption that the humanity manifest in Jesus Christ is, at the very least, the central point of reference for our thinking about the nature, capacity, and destiny of human beings as such. Classically, Christians have held and preached in common that God is united with Jesus of Nazareth in a direct and decisive manner; that in Jesus, truly divine and truly human', we are granted to see both the nature of God as unreservedly compassionate and generous, and the glory of human nature as it wholeheartedly responds to God. And this confession is not a metaphysical conclusion in the abstract, but is bound up with the experience of drastically new human possibilities that arise out of the history of Jesus.

74 But many would add that particular human beings experience such renewal outside the world of Christian tradition, and even in the context of other religious confessions. If this is so, however, the Christian is still bound to say that it is only by reference to Christ that the experience itself is possible. We do not intend here to attempt a resolution of these issues, but to indicate what is in fact the unavoidable structure of Christian judgement. We are not in a position either to state categorically that saving grace is wholly inconceivable outside the number of those who explicitly confess the name of Christ, or to adopt an easy indifferentism, for which one model of human destiny is automatically as satisfactory as any other. Once again, we are to beware of static and generalizing solutions: the degree to which we can recognize a certain 'Christlikeness' in contexts other than the Christian church depends upon the actual events of encounter and exchange between particular Christians and non-Christians.

75 The *third* variety of relativism is perhaps least complex. Christianity is a faith with historical foundations, and this means that we cannot properly talk about Jesus and his work in any way we choose. The events at the origin of the Christian community – the 'agenda' set by Jesus living, dying, and rising – are what basically and primarily establish the distinctiveness of that community. The church is a body of people living under the sign of cross and resurrection, judging and understanding themselves in this light. This is what the church proclaims itself to be when it performs the sacraments of baptism and eucharist and reads the Scriptures; without these things, there would be no body recognizable as the 'church'.

76 If so, variety in Christian utterance cannot be unlimited; it is limited by its 'charter of foundation', the event of Jesus Christ. This event, of course, is perceivable only through the medium of that primary witness which we call Holy Scripture: both record of and response to God's act, it marks out authoritatively the ground on which distinctively Christian speech and interaction occur. It is itself a variegated witness, far from monolithic, yet it is held together, in a way not always easy to spell out, by its relation to the story of a particular community and then of a particular human being and his effect in remaking and expanding that community to embrace the ends of the earth. Christian theological debate cannot but take place in the presence of this central testimony of faith, and in the confidence that it is indeed *faithful* testimony.

77 But human responses to this testimony have varied enormously, and continue to do so. This variety is not a tragedy or a problem to be overcome; it witnesses precisely to the scope, the strangeness, and the mystery of that transforming event which lies at the root of the church's

existence. 'Doing justice' to Christ and to Scripture must therefore involve the continuing meeting – and sometimes even collision – of differing perspectives and interests, a meeting which entails a continuing enlargement of horizons. We engage with the church's own varied history of reading the Bible, and with the multiplicity of contemporary readings in diverse intellectual and cultural milieus, trusting that we approach the full dimensions of the reality in question only as we continue in these encounters. We do not come to see 'truth' as an object; we do not arrive at a high ground from which to comprehend the whole work of God. But our continuing exploration in dialogue and listening rests on the trust that, so long as we go on sharing the common ground of attentiveness to the scriptural witness and sacramental fellowship, the truth of God's dealings will be with us as a hidden pulse or rhythm in all our reflection, or (to change the metaphor) as the unseen pivot in the endless oscillations of Christian debate and self-understanding. The Holy Spirit, who guides into all truth, may be present not so much exclusively on one side of a theological dispute as in the very encounter of diverse visions held by persons or groups of persons who share a faithfulness and commitment to Christ and each other.

78 In our rejection of each of the varieties of relativism mentioned, we have ended up by saying that there is indeed a 'sovereign' truth, something beyond our fashions and fancies, but that it is to be known only in the continuation of active human encounter. It is this that we mean to point to when we speak of 'pluralism'. If relativism denies that the notion of truth has any comprehensive meaning, pluralism, in the sense intended here, testifies to a truth more comprehensive than all our particular standpoints. And in Christian terms, to the extent that we remain bound in a narrow loyalty to our given

perspective, imagining it to be final, 'objective', or 'scientific', we keep truth, life-giving truth, at a distance. We can only begin from faith and commitment (in 'secular' as much as in 'religious' encounters); but that faith is challenged and enlarged in listening. If we refuse such listening, we need to be called by the Gospel to conversion and repentance, renewed attention to the Gospel and to one another in the presence of the Gospel.

79 What is essential, then, in the processes of interpretation by which the church makes judgements is an attitude which is analogous to – and may even be a part of – the repentance which the Lord called for in all his disciples. That the Scriptures speak in a variety of social situations and cultural contexts is a sign to us that the risen Christ and the Kingdom which he represents are indeed the transcendent horizon of every human society and culture, and that the bias of each particular tradition can bring into focus the meaning of God's Kingdom in a way which requires serious and critical attention. That such contexts not only illuminate but also narrow and distort the scriptural message is a sign that the risen Christ and the Kingdom he represents are indeed, in every context, a *transcendent* horizon, apprehended only by way of 'change of mind', repentance. The church grasps the Scriptures and is grasped by its Lord not apart from the challenges and dissonances which pluralism occasions, but in the repentance which these call for and make possible. The discovery of God's will or God's way is an enterprise for *historical* beings; it takes place as we grow, move, and discover ourselves and our world in *time*, the time in which God's Word has addressed us through Jesus Christ.

8 Repentance and the Variety of Religious Cultures

80 These considerations give some guidance for our churches as they approach the questions which have been raised about the 'indigenization' of Christian faith in previously non-Christian cultures. To be sure, they are far too general to resolve issues which are specific to any particular place or culture; but the key principle of what we have called 'repentance' provides a regulative norm. 'Repentance', it must be stressed, does not in this context simply mean a general willingness to take on 'new' ideas or a settled disposition to prefer the unfamiliar to the familiar. It means the change of mind which is evoked by the manifestation of God's reign in the crucified and risen Christ. Hence it means repentance on the basis both of faith in Christ and of commitment to the institutions – Scriptures, creeds, and sacraments – through which such faith is evoked and enlivened. No more than faith itself can repentance surrender its own foundations.

81 One of these foundations is the acknowledgement in faith that there is no human culture in which Christ and the Gospel of the Kingdom cannot be received, and therefore that there is, as we have said, that in every culture which answers to Christ. The doctrine of creation testifies that no people is a stranger to God or to the Christ in whom all things consist. Furthermore, the fruits of the Spirit, which are a foretaste of the Kingdom, can be – and we know this because in fact they *are* – manifested in the medium of the language, ethos, and mind-set of widely differing traditions. And since the first work of repentance is to acknowledge the signs of the Kingdom in this world for what they are, where that occurs faith will greet it with rejoicing – even if the language is

50

strange, even if the face of Christ is lit up from an unaccustomed angle.

82 In the first instance, then, repentance discerns and acknowledges, in each cultural world or medium in which the Gospel is heard and bears fruit, the continuities between the faith which is received and the medium which receives it. That such continuities exist is attested simply by the fact that the Gospel can be heard and lived by people whose sensibilities and outlook have been shaped in that setting. To discern them, moreover, is to recognize that God has borne witness to himself in the traditions – including the religious traditions – which have formed the culture in question. This judgement does not apply to some settings and not to others. The cultural worlds whose 'reason' has, in various ways, shaped the tradition of western Christianity – those of Palestinian Judaism, of Roman Hellenism, of the Celtic, Germanic, and Slavic civilizations – must be included in this judgement, together with the ancient cultures of Africa, the Americas, and the East. Christian faith also takes shape in the matrix of the industrial and technological culture which grew out of the European Enlightenment: in this secularized world too one must seek to discern testimonies – openings for faith – which illumine the meaning of God's Kingdom. Christian faith takes – and rightly takes – forms which reflect the genius of each of these 'ways'. Where there is not engagement between the Gospel and the culture, the Gospel neither takes root nor is illumined and interpreted for others.

83 But there is also a second aspect of the life of repentance. If the first is to discern and acknowledge the signs of God's Kingdom which the Gospel uncovers in every culture, and which in their turn testify to the truth which is in Christ, the second is to recognize that no human way of seeing and living

is adequate to the transcendent reality of God's Kingdom. If every culture receives and illumines the Gospel, every culture is also challenged and judged by its promise. Christian faith comes to belong to its cultural world – as much by the way it speaks *to* the world as by the way it speaks *from* it. Without belonging, it can say nothing; but its way of belonging is always that of a life which points 'beyond' – to the transcendent hope which relativizes every culture. Churches of the 'first world' have shown a marked tendency to let this truth escape them and so to fall into a kind of idolatry – to exchange, as St. Paul says in his very concrete way, 'the glory of the immortal God for images resembling mortal man' (Rom. 1.23). But such idolatry, as the Apostle argues, is the very root of sin. No culture embodies or defines in itself the meaning of God's Kingdom in Christ.

84 As, then, there are two aspects of the repentance which marks the way to God's Kingdom, so there are two sides to the 'indigenization' of the Gospel. The life in Christ belongs in every culture and transcends every culture. The church, therefore, as a sign of that, points beyond both its culture and itself to the horizon of hope which gives meaning to both.

9 Repentance and Movements for Liberation

85 The principle of repentance makes it essential to take heed of movements for social, political, and economic liberation – particularly but not exclusively in the Third World – and of the theologies which have grown up with them. Among these are the Latin American theologies of liberation, African and Black theologies, Asian theologies, feminist theologies, and others. As we have seen, these movements appeal to a certain kind of shared experience – the experience of oppression and degradation and the struggle to overcome it – as the context in which the faithful may learn the concrete meaning of God's Kingdom. The struggles of the poor and the marginalized for full human dignity, for freedom and justice, are themselves seen as signs of the Kingdom, signs of God actively present in this world, both sustaining and challenging his people. To seek God's Kingdom and his righteousness will therefore involve concerned and appropriate participation in such struggles for social, economic, and political change as make for authentic humanity in community. To stand aloof from such concern is to deny the claims upon us of God's sovereignty.

86 'Liberation theology' has, for many people, come to suggest an uncritical adoption of Marxist methods and goals. Three points need to be emphasized: first, there is, as we have indicated, a considerable variety among the theologies that have arisen out of the experience of oppression; second, not all of these find Marxist analysis and rhetoric relevant to their situation; and third, even those that do use Marxist concepts and language are not in any sense committed to an identification of the Christian hope with any variety of materialist aspiration, let alone any form of totalitarianism. They are, however, wholly committed to bringing the light and the

judgement of the Gospel to bear upon the political and economic life of mankind.

87 Fundamentally, then, these theologies of liberation are themselves a call for repentance. They testify that the struggles against injustice and inhumanity in certain structures of society are a sign of God's Kingdom which calls for 'change of mind'. Hence they have a message not only for disadvantaged societies but also for materially more comfortable nations, where relative prosperity serves to camouflage or to rationalize less obvious but still serious forms of inhumanity. Where churches are concerned, this call is also a challenge to perceive and acknowledge the social and political bearing of the Gospel and to reassess established theologies. From the perspective of the theologies of liberation, much traditional theology appears to function as little more than ideology – rationalization of the existing social order – and thus to be hostile to essential change.

88 These challenges demand serious attention. In the modern era, the proposition is often advanced that 'religion and politics don't mix'. If this statement is taken to deny that religious commitments and political attitudes are often correlated, it is manifestly false, as any historian or sociologist could testify. Similarly, if it is taken to deny that God's sovereignty extends over all areas of human life, it is theologically indefensible. Even when they refuse to 'talk politics', moreover, official and unofficial church groups engage in tacit political action by giving effective consent to the established state of affairs. Finally, it is difficult to find any nation where there are not groups of Christians actively engaged in the pursuit of social aims by political means. The question, then, is not whether religion and politics mix. It is whether churches are prepared to acknowledge, first, that the

Gospel is addressed to human beings in the social as well as the individual dimension of their lives; and second, that the Scriptures – and Christian tradition as well – evince a firm, if frequently ignored, bias in favour of the underprivileged and the put-upon. Indeed the Scriptures teach us to praise God on the ground that 'he has put down the mighty from their thrones, and exalted those of low degree' (Luke 1.52).

89 In focusing upon these truths, then, theologians of liberation and the movements they represent have not only called attention to the fact that justice and righteousness, like sin, are social and structural as well as personal and individual. They have also revealed to churches everywhere the obligation of believers to signify God's Kingdom for the world by action which makes space for justice to be done; and this means taking the side of those upon whom social and political systems inflict injustice, no matter who or what such persons happen to be in a particular society.

90 In contemporary movements for liberation, then, it is right to recognize, in the light of Scripture and of Christian tradition, a sign of God's Kingdom, and a sign which summons to repentance. At the same time, once this principle is asserted and granted, it is neither unreasonable nor faithless to notice that these movements raise theological and practical issues of great difficulty – as discussions in the Commission have revealed.

91 Liberation theologies have been charged with identifying Christian redemption with the accomplishment of their political and social aims and thus jeopardizing its transcendent dimension and its relevance to whole realms of human experience and concern which are not focused on political issues. Again, there is a difficulty occasioned by the fact that

churches are not constituted as political action groups or as political parties, but as communities which include all sorts and ages of human persons and embrace every type of human interest, from education and nurture to art and thought. Furthermore, churches as churches do not have a detailed social or economic programme to offer; they invite human beings to share and grow in a kind of life – the life in Christ. This allegiance ranges them on the side of those whom the world forgets and despises; but it provides them with no specific recipe for thought and action which can be uniformly applied in all circumstances, and hence with no licence to tie the name of God to any type of political or social system as a matter of principle. In practice, and in a particular set of circumstances, it may be perfectly clear what aims Christians are called to forward and what moral stand they are called to take – as, for example, in racist societies. Circumstances and issues, however, differ from place to place, and the available tools of social analysis are not – in spite of the claims of those who sell the several brands of them – so sharp and exact or so scientifically objective as to make decisions about the conditions which foster justice and freedom easy or self-evident. The righteousness of a cause is not in itself a guarantee either of the soundness of the methods adopted to pursue it or of the desirability of the results which those methods can achieve.

92 Such reflections underscore the seriousness and critical rigour with which Christians must answer the call of God to responsible action in the social order. The same spirit of repentance which acknowledges the call of God's Kingdom in the struggle of the oppressed for justice will also refuse to identify God's Kingdom with any human system which promises, or professes to have provided, justice once and for all. The object of the Christian faith – God's Kingdom in

Christ – is manifested and anticipated in the world; but it also stands as the world's 'beyond', as an absolute future. Hence the commitment of believers to the cause of the oppressed and the downtrodden is a continuing critical commitment which on the one hand can – and indeed must – accept relative solutions and, on the other, can never rest content with any achievement. The Kingdom of God is a principle both of affirmation and of challenge.

10 The Church and the Mystery of God's Kingdom

93   In all this, we must not lose sight of an issue internal to the life of Anglican churches. It has been the boast – and not infrequently the achievement – of churches in the Anglican tradition to encompass differing styles of piety, differing idioms in theology, and differing agenda for Christian witness and action. At times this has been accomplished only at the cost of vagueness in teaching, refusal to address fundamental theological issues, and a settled bias against serious and rigorous theological thinking. It remains true, however, that there is a legitimate – and indeed a necessary – place in Christian life for pluriformity; and it has been the genius of Anglicanism to recognize this in practice, even if Anglicans have not always troubled themselves to reflect critically on the grounds and limits of such pluriformity.

94   Both the common experience and the shared reflection of this Commission have served to bring this truth strongly home to us. If the church, because it lives 'in Christ' by the grace and power of the Holy Spirit, is a sign and agent of God's Kingdom in and for the world, it is so – always and necessarily – in a radically 'located' fashion. The church exists in particular places and at particular times, and the truth which its life and action carry is conveyed only to the extent that it too is 'located'. This means, as we have seen, that Christians in a given place and time both will and must share the cultural idiom of their geographical and social locale. It also means that their life and witness both will and must address the issues, moral and political, with which historical circumstance confronts them in that locale. The church belongs to all its many places and times, and it is in this fact that its legitimate pluriformity is, in the end, rooted.

95 'Belonging' and pluralism: these are centuries-old, correlative marks of the Anglican spirit, which has always sought to speak in 'a tongue understanded of the people', and which still seeks to do so even when 'the people' speaks, much more obviously than in the past, in many tongues. It is natural and appropriate, therefore, that the Anglican Communion today should take the form of a fellowship that encourages local and regional initiative and nourishes styles of church life which fit – and address – particular societies and cultures.

96 The church, however, does not have the source and principle of its life in any one society or culture or in any group of them. It lives only in and from that transcendent 'horizon' of human life which is the Kingdom of God as realized in the risen Christ, and it exists to be a sign of that Kingdom in and for the many social and cultural 'places' in which it lives. For this reason, there can be no careless or unqualified affirmation of 'belonging' and of pluralism, even for Anglicans. It is not enough to speak a language 'understanded of the people'; that language, whether spoken or acted, must convey, in its place, the 'beyond' of God's grace and judgement in Christ. The idiom may be – indeed it *is* – manifold; but still 'there is one body and one Spirit, just as you were called to the one hope that belongs to your call, one Lord, one faith, one baptism, one God and Father of us all, who is above all and through all and in all' (Eph. 4.4–6).

97 This unity is found, in the first instance, precisely through the continuing fellowship of churches that belong in different places. For Anglicans, such fellowship is based in a common set of institutions: Scriptures, ecumenical creeds, sacraments, the historic threefold ministry. It comes to practical expression, however, through practical acts of sharing,

through mutual consultation, and through mutual admonition and criticism. We have already argued that pluralism can serve the cause of a deeper and fuller understanding of the Gospel and so of a deeper and fuller unity in Christ; but it can do so only on the condition that churches do not eschew their responsibility to one another, a responsibility that includes hearing as well as speaking, learning as well as teaching. And this in turn can only occur, in the Anglican Communion, through a common willingness to take up difficult – even divisive – issues for the sake of the truth of the Gospel. For too long Anglicans have appeared willing to evade responsible theological reflection and dialogue by acquiescing automatically and immediately in the co-existence of incompatible views, opinions, and policies.

98 To affirm pluralism, then, is to affirm not one but two things. On the one hand it means to assert that there is good in the existence and continuing integrity of a variety of traditions and ways of life; on the other hand, it means to assert that there is good in their interplay and dialogue. For Christians, moreover, such affirmation of pluralism has a special meaning. It embodies a recognition that every human culture has God's Kingdom as its horizon in creation and redemption. At the same time, it acknowledges that, in the dialogue between traditions, people's understanding of the meaning of God's Kingdom, and of the Christ who bears it, may be enhanced. Pluralism, when understood in this way, is a stimulus to the repentance by which believers discern and turn to God's Kingdom.

99 It is important to reiterate, however, that the stimulus to repentance is not the same as its ground. It is not pluralism, but the risen Christ as the bearer of God's reign, who is the ground of Christian repentance as well as of Christian faith,

because he is the one in whom the unity of humankind is established and promised. Pluralism is to be affirmed not as it divides people, and not as a recipe for indifferentism, but as the context in which the heirs of God's Kingdom may engage with one another more richly and variously than hitherto and may thus be enabled the better to know and to follow Christ – the Second Adam, the new humanity – who embodies the mystery of God's Kingdom, and into whom all are called to 'grow up'.

APPENDIX 1

Papers Prepared for the Commission

Christian Identity in Cultural Context
Bishop Lakshman Wickremesinghe

Real Presence
Image of God
Helen Oppenheimer

Liberation and the Political and Social Dimension
Dr Rowan Williams

Kingdom and Church: Some Preliminary Notes
Dr Richard A Norris Jr

Creation in the Bible and Tradition
Professor John Pobee

Theology of Liberation in Latin America
Dr Jaci Maraschin

Sin and Evil in Creation
Redemption and the Cross
Dr Helen Milton

The Church in Liberation Theology
Canon Sehon Goodridge

The Gospel and Context
Canon J Hartin

The Church in Relation to the Kingdom
Archbishop Donald Robinson

The Secularization of Christianity
Archbishop Keith Rayner

The Church in Relation to the Kingdom
Canon Martin Mbwana

Creation, Fall, and Redemption
The Revd George Braund

Christian Identity in Cultural Context
Archdeacon George Connor

APPENDIX 2

Members of the Commission

The Revd Canon Dr Alan Chor-Choi Chan   Hong Kong
Lecturer, Chung Chi College

The Venerable George H.D. Connor   New Zealand
Archdeacon of Waiapu, formerly Lecturer,
Theological College, Kohimarama, Solomon Islands

The Revd Canon Sehon Goodridge   Barbados
Warden/Student Counsellor of the University of the
West Indies Cave Hill Campus, Barbados, formerly
Principal of Codrington College, the Provincial
Theological College

The Revd Canon James Hartin   Ireland
Principal of the Church of Ireland Theological College,
Dublin and Professor of Pastoral Theology, Trinity College
Dublin

The Revd Dr Jaci C. Maraschin   Brazil
Lecturer, Associação de Seminarios Theologicos
Evangélicos, São Paulo

The Revd Canon Martin Mbwana   Tanzania
Canon Chancellor of Diocese of Zanzibar and Tanga and
formerly Warden, St Mark's Theological College,
Dar es Salaam

Dr Helen Milton   Canada
Formerly Lecturer, University of Windsor, Ontario

The Revd Dr Richard A. Norris Jr   United States of
Professor of Church History,   America
Union Theological Seminary, New York

Lady Oppenheimer   England
Writer on Christian Ethics, formerly Lecturer at
Cuddesdon College, Oxford

Professor John Pobee   Ghana
Associate Director, Programme on Theological Education
of the World Council of Churches, formerly
Professor of New Testament and Church History,
University of Ghana at Legon

The Most Revd Keith Rayner (Chairman)   Australia
Archbishop of Adelaide

The Most Revd Donald W.B. Robinson   Australia
Archbishop of Sydney

The Revd Dr Rowan Williams   Wales
University Lecturer and Dean of Clare College,
Cambridge

The Rt Revd Lawrence Zulu   South Africa
Bishop of Zululand

The Rt Revd Lakshman Wickremesinghe   Sri Lanka
Bishop of Kurunagala
(First two meetings)